COSMIC

CANNABIS

CONSCIOUSNESS

VOLUME I

Compiled by Ann Nelson
find me in the Twittersphere
@Philosopher2084

Copyright @ 2018
The scanning, uploading and distribution of the contents of this publication via the Internet or any other means is perfectly okay by me, without prior written permission. **Blaze free.**

INTRODUCTION

We have been waiting for you. We're glad you're here as we search for the secrets at the heart of time and space. As purveyors of the red pill, we'll be exploring the ultimate quest for knowledge from the spaceless realm through the ancient wisdom traditions to the science of human consciousness.

Everything is consciousness. The substance of the universe is consciousness. Dark matter is quantum soup. It's as if we are still in the cosmic dark ages when it comes to the brain, mind, soul, Soul, Higher Self, Divine Intelligence and Cosmic Consciousness.

When those edibles finally kick in, we'll seek to disentangle our experience of reality and reach higher consciousness through our curriculum in Earth School. You are a quantum reality ~ a you-niverse ~ and are awakening to the supra conscious — an exalted elevated existence. We'll experience the astounding positive potential of the cannabis high as a tool to exploration and discovery.

I have been exploring spirituality and consciousness my whole life and attended the Council Grove Conference on Altered States of Consciousness for 23 years. In 1991, I chaired the annual conference sponsored by the Menninger Foundation and The Life Sciences Institute of Mind Body Health. For one week every year, we gathered on the Kansas prairie to discuss voluntary controls as well as altered states of consciousness.

Since 1968, world pioneers in all areas of science have gathered to share their work in the cosmic realm on the subtle energies of life, states of consciousness and spiritual evolution. Their focus is developing common perceptions of the fundamental issues related to understanding consciousness, be it physical, mental, emotional, transpersonal or extrapersonal; leading to the possibility of a Science of Consciousness.

What I know for certain is that something major is happening. We are waking up to enlightening epiphanies, enigmas and esoteric wisdom as never before in our history. Perhaps it is a world we can't see, but the paradigm-shifting potential of cannabis may lead us to authentic self-realization and lead us to deeper insights and inner transformation.

Welcome aboard. Keep blazing and stay amazing. We are all cosmic consciousness conductors in our transcendent biodegradable spacesuits and this may be our vehicle to cosmic awareness, awakening and astounding positive cannabis highs.

Keep on thinking free. Keep this book close…it is recommended for keeping on your bedside table to open at random before drifting from lights-off theta-state thoughts into etheric danked dreams. You'll be glad you did.

Now find a lighter and turn on some mind-altering music…

*I'd like to dedicate this to all
the creator's righteous children...
I have some food in my bag for you.
Not the edible food — the food you eat?
No.*

*Have some food for thought,
Since knowledge is infinite,*

It has infinitely fell on me...

erykah badu

We invite you, in reading this book,
to cast away your preconceptions and enter,
with us, a magical world where all things
are connected to you, and you are
connected to all things.

sun bear
The Medicine Wheel

Once upon a time the gods gathered and decided to send yet another mission to Planet Earth. A briefing was held to prepare for the descent. Those that would go chose to become human and would have to lose all memory of their divinity. Their task would be to discover one another on Earth, recover their memories through intuition, and piece together the members of the descent.

In the darkness that covered the earth, these individuals and sacred places were points of scattered light in a web which bound the dark: a scattering of people, a light webby tension of them everywhere over the globe.

william irwin thompson

Nobody comes into your life by mere coincidence.
Trust your instincts.
Do the unexpected. Find the others.

timothy leary

The awakening has begun.
We are entering a whole new age,
a whole new frequency, a whole new
vibration. Never before have we seen
such a quantum leap in the evolution of
consciousness for Humanity and
Mother Earth.

tim zyphin

The awakening of consciousness
is the next evolutionary step for mankind.

eckhart tolle

electromagnetic noise

*We are controlling transmission…
do not adjust your TV… You are about to
experience the awe and mystery which reaches
from the inner mind to the outer limits…
There is nothing wrong with your
television… Sit quietly and we will control
all that you see there.*

The Outer Limits

You do not need to leave your room.
Remain sitting at your table and listen.
Do not even listen, simply wait, be quite
still and solitary.The world will freely offer
itself to you to be unmasked, it has no
choice, it will roll in ecstasy at your feet.

franz kafka

The Architect: Hello, Neo.

Neo: Who are you?

The Architect: I am the Architect. I created the Matrix. I've been waiting for you. You have many questions, and although the process has altered your consciousness, you remain irrevocably human. Ergo, some of my answers you will understand, and some of them you will not.
Concordantly, while your first question may be the most pertinent, you may or may not realize it is also the most irrelevant.

The Matrix Reloaded

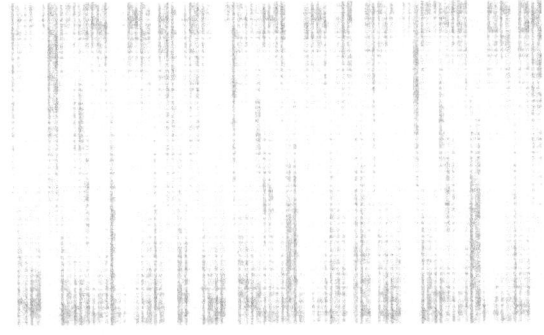

As all historians know, the past is
a great darkness, and filled with echoes.
Voices may reach from it; but what they say
to us is imbued with the obscurity of the
matrix out of which they come; and, try as
we may, we cannot always decipher them
precisely in the clearer light of our own day.

margaret atwood

Your divine essence is already in the
enlightened state. You are already free from
the bondage of imaginary suffering. You may
leave this human dream of suffering anytime
and relax into the oceanic experience of pure
unfounded consciousness. That is your
freedom.

@HiDimensions

This is where we are right now, as a whole. No one is left out of the loop. We are experiencing a reality based on a thin veneer of lies and illusions. A world where greed is our god and wisdom is a sin; where division is key and unity is fantasy; where ego-driven cleverness of the mind is praised, rather than the intelligence of the heart.

bill hicks

If you're reading this, go smoke some weed. You deserve it.

@HighVibes

All great teachers declare that within
this body is the immortal soul: I am
beyond everyday finite; I now see that the
spirit, alone in space with its ever-new joy,
has expressed itself as the vast body of
nature. I am the stars, I am the waves, I am
the life of all; I am the laughter within all
hearts, I am the wisdom and power that
sustain all creation.

yogananda

We wish you to be informed about what
you are dealing with. Light is information;
ignorance is darkness. We want you to be
working in the light, not in the dark.

the pleiadians
barbara marciniak

I live on Earth at present,
and I don't know what I am.
I know that I am not a category.
I am not a thing — a noun.
I seem to be a verb,
an evolutionary process —
an integral function of the universe.

buckminster fuller

We are the local embodiment of a Cosmos grown to self-awareness. We have begun to contemplate our origins: starstuff pondering the stars; organized assemblages of ten billion billion billion atoms considering the evolution of atoms; tracing the long journey by which, here at least, consciousness arose. Our loyalties are to the species and the planet. We speak for Earth. Our obligation to survive is owed not just to ourselves but also to that Cosmos, ancient and vast, from which we spring.

carl sagan

The beginning of freedom is the realization that you are not 'the thinker'. The moment you start watching the thinker, a higher level of consciousness has become activated. You begin to realize that there is a vast realm of intelligence beyond thought, that thought is only a time aspect of the intelligence. You also realize that all the things that truly matter ~ love, beauty, creativity, joy, inner peace arise from beyond the mind.
You begin to awaken.

eckhart tolle

To change the world is not your mission.
To change yourself is not your duty.
To awaken to your true nature is your opportunity.

mooji

Long before the awakening of thought on earth, manifestations of **cosmic energy** must have been reproduced which have no parallel today.

pierre teilhard de chardin

Become conscious of being conscious.

eckhart tolle

What lies at the very core of human consciousness?

adyashanti

The brain and body merely function as a relay station receiving part of the overall consciousness and part of our memories in measurable and constantly changing electromagnetic fields.

pim van lommels

The universe works like a grand cosmic hologram.

david bohm

*I'm just going to keep smoking
'til shit makes sense or I fall asleep.*

thegoodvibe.com

I would say in one sentence my goal is to at least be part of the journey to find the unified theory that Einstein himself was really the first to look for. He didn't find it, but we think we're hot on the trail.

brian greene

Life is a manifestation of the unified
field of consciousness.
Colors, beauty, pleasure and pain
are its songs of creation.

amit ray

The unified field is
fundamentally a field of consciousness.

maharishi mahesh yogi

The Super Conscious Mind is the
Unified Field.

elmer green
#a unified field of planetary consciousness

Human consciousness is one of the grand mysteries of our time on earth. How do you know that you are "you"? …What really happens when you enter an "altered" state of consciousness with the help of some chemical or plant? Are animals conscious? While you would think this basic enigma of our self-awareness would be at the forefront of scientific inquiry, science does not yet have strong answers to these questions.

big think

As above, so below, as within, so without, as the universe, so the soul.

hermes trismagistus

There is an unseen force, a cosmic intelligence that is taking care of everything, at every moment.

swami satchidananda

You are the universe, expressing itself as a human for a little while.

eckhart tolle

You are not a human being in search of a spiritual experience.
You are a spiritual being immersed in a human experience.

swami satchidananda

You are a timeless, spaceless, ageless being that lives inside a temporary vessel that is here for a journey of learning how to love yourself more, love the planet more and love one another more.

pleiadian love

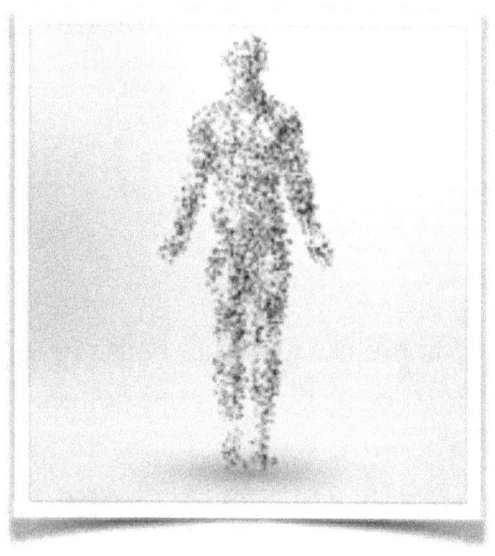

Cosmic Consciousness
is a further stage of human evolution
which will be reached by all humanity
in the future.

richard maurice bucke

If your mind is empty, it is always ready
for anything; it is open to everything.
In the beginner's mind there are many
possibilities; in the expert's mind
there are few.

shunryu suzuki

As far as we can discern, the sole purpose
of human existence is to kindle a light in
the darkness of mere being.

carl jung

*Among the great things which are
to be found among us,
the Being of Nothingness
is the greatest.*

leonardo da vinci

Consciousness may seem exceedingly elusive and subtle. For some it seems like focusing on consciousness is foolhardy and a waste of time…better to get busy making things happen. There is a time for constructive action, to be sure. However, building up one's consciousness of Life, Truth and Self is the highest order of priority and greatest key to true Power. For you are not only Love and Light; you are consciousness in expression.

dr. roger teel
This Life is Joy

The aim of spiritual life is to awaken a joyful freedom, a benevolent and compassionate heart in spite of everything.

jack kornfield

Cosmic consciousness is a higher form of consciousness than that possessed by the ordinary man. **Cosmic consciousness** is an interconnected way of seeing things which is more of an intuitive knowing than it is a factual understanding.

richard maurice bucke

We'll begin to vibrate at higher frequencies as our consciousness aligns with our Higher Self and Oneness. Ascension will raise the Consciousness of our planet. This is our mission. This is why we are here.
Here's why:

Cosmic consciousness denotes a **higher** or particularly spiritual level of awareness and consciousness…a hidden consciousness or reality which is beyond the perceivable world.

It is said that in a state of **cosmic consciousness**, the human mind is **elevated** beyond the awareness of the self and the ego, and enters a place of oneness and unity with the universe.

yogapedia

You are one of the rare people who can
separate your observation from your
preconception. You see what is,
where most people see
what they expect.

john steinbeck

*From the moment you came into the world
of being, a ladder was placed before you,
that you might escape.*

shams

There is no doubt whatsoever
that the universe is the
merest illusion.

sri ramana maharshi

Western philosophy has its origins in **conversation**, in face-to-face discussions about reality, our place in the cosmos, and how we should live. It began with a sense of mystery, wonder and confusion, and the powerful desire to get beyond mere appearances to find truth or, if not that, at least some kind of wisdom or balance.

aeon

I'm happy today.
Would you like to know why?
Because I'm baked, darling.
Like an apple pie.

themetapicture.com

*The truth was a mirror in the hands of God.
It fell, and broke into pieces.
Everybody took a piece of it, and they
looked at it
and thought they had the truth.*

rumi

The will to be who you really are
comes into your consciousness,
leading you to a new level of understanding.

matt kahn

*I quote others only in order to better express
myself.*

michel de montaigne

If you don't smoke cannabis,
you may spend your evening balancing your checking account. It you do smoke cannabis you may spend your evening contemplating the causes of the Greek Renaissance.

terence mcKenna
#Let'sgetHigh

What book would you make compulsory reading? I would punish elitist English professors by making them read Ulysses over and over until they admit that it's a long, well-written joke on literature.

orson scott card

I put the Lit in Literature

By paying attention to the way you feel, and then choosing thoughts that feel the very best, you are managing your own vibration, which means you are creating your own reality…the less attention you give to everybody else's reality, the purer your vibration is going to be — and the more you are going to be pleased with what comes to you.

abraham

Tonight
With wine being poured
And the instruments singing
Amongst themselves
One thing is forbidden
One thing…
Sleep.

rumi

I can think of no right more fundamental than the right to peacefully steward the contents of one's own consciousness.

@SamHarris.org

Matter is energy (light), whose vibration has been so lowered as to be perceptible to the senses. There is no matter.

albert einstein

Every time I find the meaning of life, *they change it…*

@euphoria

I like smoking weed in the Grand Canyon
or in the woods…It does remind you of
your space in the universe — and reframe
things for you. I think you can have
some very profound experiences.

susan sarandon

Mountain air.
The scent of pine needles.
Sitting on the bank of a mountain
stream, letting time go by.

@Basque Philosopher

I'm high on life. And weed.
Mostly weed.

someecards

I've learned to control emotions, dreams and visions. I have always cherished, as I nurtured my enthusiasm. All my long life I spent in ecstasy. That was the source of my happiness. It helped me during all these years to bear with work, which was enough for five lives. The best is to work at night, because of the stellar light, and close bond. **Everything is light.**

nikola tesla

The genius lights on his age like a comet into the paths of the planets.

arthur schopenhauer

I wanted to illuminate the whole earth. There is enough electricity to become a second sun. Light would appear around the equator, as a ring around Saturn. Mankind is not ready for the great and good. In Colorado Springs I soaked the earth by electricity. Also we can harness the other energies, such as positive mental energy. They are in the music of Bach or Mozart, or in the verses of great poets. In the Earth's interior, there are energies of Joy, Peace and Love. Their expressions are a flower that grows from the Earth, the food we get out of her and everything that makes man's homeland. I've spent years looking for the way that this energy could influence people. The beauty and the scent of roses can be used as a medicine and the sun rays as a food.

nikola tesla

Since the dawn of time we've been ignoring
the smartest people's advice from
Copernicus to Oppenheimer.
Why do we distrust intelligence?

@dorkyswallow

The speed of light: **299 792 458** M/S

Exact coordinates for The Great Pyramid:

29.9 792 458 °

#blowminding

Happiness can be found even in the darkest of times, if one only remembers to turn on the Light.

dumbledore

Happiness is the meaning and the purpose
of life, the whole aim and end of human
existence.

aristotle

Eventually,
you will come to understand
that love heals everything, and love
is all there is.

gary zukav

I'd rather write about laughing than crying,
for laughter makes men human, and
courageous.
BE HAPPY!

francois rabelais

It seems that it is impossible to live without discovering the purpose of your life. And the first thing which a person should do is to understand the meaning of life. But the majority of people who consider themselves to be educated are so proud that they have reached such great heights that they cease to care about the meaning of existence.

leo tolstoy

The mind seems to contain everything at once in a timeless and spaceless interconnectedness.

pim van lommels

hits blunt
"What if sleeping is our natural state and we're only awake to gather information for our dreams?"

#WhatDoYouMeme

If you come across information that brings your reality into question, don't attack the person providing the information research it!

@EndTimesAlert

Learning the truth comes with isolation from people. Once you learn it, you want to tell everyone, but you won't get the response you are expecting.
People are programmed to reject the truth immediately without even looking into it themselves. You may even lose friends over it.

@johnnyyash

There are two kinds of people in this world. Those that smoke weed and those that should.

Our society has been dumbed down and indoctrinated so bad they assume every critical thinker is a conspiracy theorist.

ralph smart

"We will not respond substantively to unnamed sources peddling second-hand hearsay with rank speculation that continues to leak inaccurate information."

#double talk

It's not peer pressure, it's just your turn

Very private people have mastered the art of telling you little about themselves but doing it in such a way you think you know a lot.

@What The F*** Facts

The individual has always had to struggle to keep from being overwhelmed by the tribe. If you try it, you will be lonely often, and sometimes frightened. But no price is too high to pay for the privilege of owning yourself.

nietzsche

The matrix a holographic universe being projected to us by those who wish to control us. Humanity has been suppressed and controlled in this manner for a millennium. We think it is real but in actual fact it is just a film being played to the collective consciousness presenting itself as reality. I imagine that right now, you're feeling a bit like Alice. Hm? Tumbling down the rabbit hole?

morpheus

There is only one thing you should do.
Go into yourself.

rainier maria rilke

I cannot tell you any spiritual truth
that deep within you don't know already.
All I can do is remind you of what
you have forgotten.

eckhart tolle

But do not ask me where I am going
as I travel in this limitless world;
where every step I take is my home.

doge

Smoke a blunt.
Sit under the stars.
Talk about space.

@PeaceLoveHerbs

Behind us: the unknown.
Before us: the secret.

terence mckenna

We must be willing to get rid of the life
we've planned, so as to have the life that
is waiting for us.

joseph campbell

Give up the search: there is no teacher,
no student and no teaching.

papaji

Your adventure has to be coming out of your own interior. If you are ready for it then doors will open where there were no doors before, and where there would not be doors for anyone else. And you must have courage. It's the call to adventure, which means there is no security, no rules.

joseph campbell

You are a timeless, spaceless, ageless being that lives inside a temporary vessel that is here for a journey of learning how to love yourself more, love the planet more and love one another more.

pleiadian love

The softest thing in the universe overcomes the hardest thing in the universe. That without substance can enter where there is no room. Hence I know the value of non-action.

lao tzu

We go through life walking in the immense darkness of unknown realities with a little flashlight.

adyashanti

Long before the awakening of thought
on earth, manifestations of
cosmic energy
must have been reproduced which
have no parallel today.

pierre teilhard de chardin

According to Vedanta, there are only
two symptoms of enlightenment…
a higher consciousness:

The first symptom is that you stop
worrying. Things don't bother you anymore.
You become light-hearted and full of joy.

The second symptom is that
you encounter more and more meaningful
coincidences in your life, more and more
synchronicities.

And this accelerates to the point where
you actually experience the miraculous.

deepak chopra

Consciousness-one level is understanding.
Consciousness-two is where we understand
our position in society: who's top dog,
who's underdog and who's in the middle.
And Type-three consciousness is simulating
in the future. And Type-three consciousness ~
only humans have this ability to see far into
the future.

michio kaku

If I find in myself a desire which no
experience in this world can satisfy,
the most probable explanation is that
I was made for another world.

c.s. lewis

For the unconscious psyche, space and time seem to be relative; that is to say, knowledge finds itself in a space-time continuum in which space is no longer space, nor time time. If, therefore, the unconscious should develop or maintain a potential in the direction of consciousness, it is then possible for parallel events to be perceived or "known".

carl jung

*"Nothing would be what it is
because everything would be what it isn't.
And contrary-wise; what it is it wouldn't be,
and what it wouldn't be, it would. You see?"*

alice in wonderland

Earth is a realm it is not a planet. It is not an object, therefore, it has no edge. Earth would be more easily defined as a system environment. Earth is also a machine, it is a Tesla coil. The sun and moon are powered wirelessly with the electromagnetic fields. This field also suspends the celestial spheres with electromagnetic levitation. Electromagnetic levitation disproves gravity because the only force you need to counter is the electromagnetic force, not gravity. The stars are attached to the firmament.

nikola tesla

You'll see it when
you believe it.

wayne dyer

*Cosmic Consciousness
resonates everywhere,
in everything.*

Consciousness…is returning to the
center of reality, acting, as all the Mystics
throughout history have told us, as the
'vehicle of existence,' while the universe
begins to appear "more like a great thought
than as a great machine." Physicists now
theorize that consciousness is actually
'embedded' into the structure of the
universe or even that reality is conscious,
as the Hindus, Buddhists and many other
ancient cultures have believed…

james oroc

Some say that individuality is an illusion. I think it is better understood that each person is an island in a sea of islands all bounded and thus connected by a vast ocean which is **cosmic consciousness.**

parker stafford

I am no longer the wave of consciousness thinking itself separated from the sea of **cosmic consciousness**. I am the ocean of Spirit that has become the wave of human life.

yogananda

Stoners are deeply philosophical people,
always trying to understand and interpret
the world we live in, and being high
broadens our minds and enables us to gain
full respect of the beauty in our world.

urban dictionary

We are a group
where the greathearted gather.
We are a door that's never locked.
If you are suffering any kind of pain,
stay near this door.
Open it.

rumi

You have to grow from the inside out.
None can teach you, none can make you
spiritual. There is no other teacher but
your own Soul.

swami vivekananda

At some point, we break through into
a whole new dimension of consciousness.

adyashanti

Soon the child's clear eye is clouded
over by ideas and opinions,
preconceptions and abstractions.
Simple free being becomes encrusted
with the burdensome armor to the ego.
Not until years later does an
instinct come that a vital sense of
mystery has been withdrawn. The sun
glints through the pines, and the heart is
pierced in a moment of beauty and
strange pain, like a memory of paradise.

After that day…
we become seekers.

peter matthiessen

Conscious choice and careful articulation
can move us toward a more perfect
reflection of the best possibilities,
perhaps toward something divine.
Love is a phenomenon which correlates
to **human consciousness**.

But what type of love, how transformative
with the promise of the divine realization,
depends on our thought-filled will?
Seal the field…stay the course.

jay bremyer

To know someone here or there
with whom you feel there is an
understanding in spite of distances
or thought unexpressed ~
that can make of this earth a garden.

goethe

Paradise is not a place
but a state of consciousness.

@AlienBeingAlien

To me, high is a place.
And I really treasure that. I love going there. And when I want to go there, I want to go there. I don't need my government to give me a passport for that place.

rick steves, travel writer

We are all visitors to this time, this place.
We are just passing through.
Our purpose here is to observe, to learn, to grow, to love
…and then we return home.

@ThirdEyeThoughts

When we do deep inner exploration,
through our meditation and inquiry
we start to penetrate through all the
layers of identity, belief and opinion.

CIII

The mystical life is the centre of all that
I do and all that I think and all that I write.

w.b. yeats

Rave on Mr. Yeats…

van morrison

THE LAKE ISLE OF INNISFREE

I will arise and go now, and go to Innisfree,
And a small cabin there, of clay and wattles made;
Nine bean rows will I have there, a hive for the honey bee,
And live alone in the bee-loud glade.

And I shall have some peace there, for peace comes dropping slow,
Dropping from the veils of the morning to where the cricket sings;
There midnight's all a glimmer, and noon a purple glow,
And evening full of the linnet's wings.

I will arise and go now, for always, night and day,
I hear the lake-water lapping with low sounds by the shore;
While I stand on the roadway, or on the pavements gray,
I hear it in the deep heart's core.

w.b. yeats

The only thing we can control is
the direction of our consciousness.
Trying to control conditions creates a
difficult life based on fear. Higher
consciousness paves the way for more
harmonious conditions to evolve.

dr. roger teel
This life is Joy

Our life is what our consciousness
makes it.

ernest holmes

Once we believe in ourselves,
we can risk curiosity, wonder,
spontaneous delight or an experience
that reveals the human spirit.

e.e. cummings

The will to be who you really are
comes into your consciousness,
leading you to a new level
of understanding.

matt kahn

*How do you know when you are stoned?
When you are too phoned to stone home.*

i thank you god
for most this amazing day:
for the leaping greenly spirits of trees
and a blue true dream of sky;
and for everything
which is natural
which is infinite
*which is **yes**...*

now the ears of my ears awake
and
now the eyes of my eyes are opened.

e.e. cummings

*Your happy heart brings joy and
peace where there is none*

If your mind is empty,
it is always ready for anything; it is open
to everything. In the beginner's mind
there are many possibilities; in the
expert's mind there are few.

shunryu suzuki

*The truth was a mirror
in the hands of God.
It fell, and broke into pieces.
Everybody took a piece of it,
and they looked at it and
thought they had the truth.*

rumi

Your divine essence is already in the enlightened state. You are already free from the bondage of imaginary suffering. You may leave this human dream of suffering anytime and relax into the oceanic experience of pure unfounded consciousness.
That is your freedom.

@HiDimensions

*Whenever we pause, and enter the quiet
and rest in the utter stillness,*

*We can hear that whispering voice
calling to us still;
never forget the Good,
and never forget the True,
and never forget the Beautiful,*

*for these are the faces
of your own deepest Self,
freely shown to you.*

ken wilber

I am no longer the wave of
consciousness thinking itself separated
from the sea of **cosmic consciousness**.
I am the ocean of Spirit that has
become the wave of human life.

yogananda

The awakening has begun.
We are entering a whole new age,
a whole new frequency, a whole new
vibration. Never before have we seen
such a quantum leap in the evolution
of consciousness for Humanity and
Mother Earth.

tim zyphin

You have to grow from the inside out.
None can teach you, none can make you
spiritual. There is no other teacher but
your own Soul.

swami vivekananda

The #1 way to spend your 'high time' :

Being stoned, alone in the dark,
listening to music with your headphones
on or your stereo turned up obscenely loud,
is nothing less than a spiritual experience.
You can feel the bass vibrating in your cells,
and see colorful patterns conjured up on the
back of your closed eyelids shifting and
dancing in time with the song.

You can leave the whole world behind
and lose yourself in lush and vivid inner
dimensions; you can be moved to tears
and laughter, and have life-changing
epiphanies, as the music ebbs and
flows and unveils deeper prayers,
and hidden meanings.

@weedreader

Cannabis enables non-musicians to know a little about what it is like to be a musician, and non-artists to grasp the joys of art.

carl sagan

Smoking weed doesn't make you cool, but if you're cool, you probably smoke weed.

Stoners are deeply philosophical people,
always trying to understand and interpret
the world we live in, and being high
broadens our minds and enables us to
gain full respect of the beauty in our world.

urban dictionary

Another wonder of cannabis
is that it can improve the 'energy body'.
It expands your consciousness!
This is why it has always been
considered a **sacred herb.**

the mind unleashed

Cannabis is one of the oldest
and best medicines known to man:

PTSD
ADHD
cancer
asthma
tinnitus
diabetes
shingles
anorexia
migraine
psoriasis
insomnia
glaucoma
eases gout
fibromyalgia
atherosclerosis
crohn's disease
treats alcoholism
multiple sclerosis
fights free radicals
opioid dependence
slows inflammation
rheumatoid arthritis
prevents Alzheimer's
cardiovascular disease
stimulates bone growth
suppresses muscle spasm
controls epileptic seizures
everything except stupidity
and much more

Marijuana grows brain cells.

#neurogenesis

WEED:
It's like taking an anti-depressant,
an anti-anxiety pill, a sleeping pill,
a muscle relaxant and a personal
therapist, and rolling them all into one.

WeedClub.com

In Colorado yesterday, voters approved a tax on marijuana to fund the building of schools. In other words, kids, don't do drugs, but stay in the schools funded by them.

conan

A day without pot is like, school.

Colorado voted to legalize
the recreational use of marijuana.
The new state slogan is:
"Come for the legal marijuana,
Stay because you forgot to leave.

jimmy kimmel

Philosophy should be conversation, not
dogma — face-to-face talk about our place
in the cosmos and how we should live.
Without conversation philosophy
is just dogma.

nigel warburton

History of epistemology:

- 300 BC: you can't know anything
- 600 BC: some stuff you can't know
- 1600 BC: no, not even that
- 1800 BC: what about this?
- 2000 BC: no

@existentialcoms

If you think you're free, there's no escape possible.

ram dass

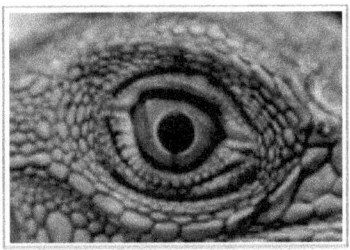

La vida humana tiene tan solo
el objetivo y la meta que el individuo
le asigna.

rudolph steiner

Carpe diem.
As we speak time is running away
from us. Seize the day,
don't put your faith in the future.

@New Philosopher

People don't realize that the future
is just now, but later.

russell brand

You are an aperture
through which the universe is
looking at and exploring itself.

alan watts

From the multi-sensory point of view;
insights, intuitions, hunches and
inspirations are messages from Soul,
or from advanced intelligences.

@Immortal Masters

The soul is a god memory.

hopi white

We are not born into the world.
We are born into something
that we make into the world.

michael talbot

It is not we who create, but universal
intelligence that creates through us.

eckhart tolle

The world you perceive is made of
consciousness; what you call matter
is consciousness itself.

nisargadatta maharaj

The universe is determined
by vibrational frequencies
in the heart of every single particle.

@Immortal Masters

The amount of time it takes you to get from where you want to be, is only the amount of time it takes you to change the vibration within you. Instant manifestation could be yours if you could instantly change the vibration.

abraham

From the body electric, to the human aura, Einstein's field equations, and the 9 rings of **cosmic consciousness**;
human beings' thoughts and feelings
are more powerful than radio transmissions.

david sereda

To rise in consciousness to the level
of the thing desired and to remain there
until such level becomes your nature is
the way of all seeming miracles.

neville goddard

The man of **cosmic consciousness**, never feeling himself as limited to a body or as reaching only to the brain, or only to the cerebral-lotus light of a thousand rays, instead feels by true intuitive power the ever-bubbling Bliss that dances in every particle of his little body, and in his big Cosmic Body of the universe, and in his absolute nature as one with the Eternal Spirit beyond manifested forms.

paramahansa yogananda

What is it like to be high on marijuana? Can cannabis highs help you to remember long gone events, to fuel your imagination, to work creatively, to come to introspective and other insights, to empathically understand others, and to personally grow? How much did cannabis inspire outstanding thinkers, artists and musicians like Charles Baudelaire, Rudyard Kipling, Walter Benjamin, Billie Holiday, Diego Rivers, John Lennon, Carl Sagan, and so many others? And how much did the marijuana high positively transform our society?

sebastian marincolos

[What is it like to be high on marijuana?]:

I use two vape pens to hold my man bun
in place while I rollerblade.

gian d'oh

Listen: there's a hell of a good universe
next door:
let's go!

e.e. cummings

When I think about the people
I have smoked pot with,
they're such an eclectic mix of people,
and I probably never would have
spoken to a lot of them if it weren't for
pot. Alcohol doesn't bring people
together like that.

dave chappelle

There is something so unbelievably
refreshing about meeting individuals
who are on the same life frequency as you.
Everything feels effortless and natural.
You just vibe, it's fucking beautiful.

Soul Healing Wisdom

We are really advocates of just getting as happy as you can be — which takes care of everything. Even if you don't have reason to be happy ~ make it up. Fantasize it. Make a decision that you're going to be happy one way or another — no matter what. I'm going to be happy.
I'm going to be happy.
I'm going to be happy.

abraham

"Happy Thanksgiving son, so what's new in the world?"

"Well, our president has joined with other leaders in a **global alliance** to stop an international satanic pedophile ring who worship an artificial intelligence who have taken over this reptilian species and use them as their muscle to conquer worlds and turn them into their subservient followers.

They implemented a plan decades ago to step up their game and introduce their AI matrix on this planet to get us all addicted to their technology and infrastructure so they could then slowly get us to willfully participate in their hive-mind neural net matrix and give up all free will."

* "Interesting. Can you pass the mashed potatoes?"

I'll take
"Things You Never Ever Never Ever
Ever Never Thought You'd Hear"
for $100 Alex.

dennis miller

Those who cannot understand
how to put their thoughts on ice
should not enter into the heat of debate.

friedrich nietzsche

*I'm blunt because
God rolled me that way.*

Accidents happen, that's what everyone says. But in a quantum universe there are no such things as accidents, only possibilities and probabilities folded into existence by perception.

joseph michael straczynski

How you perceive a situation controls your genes. That means you can change your genetics by becoming a master of perception.

@MaryamHasnaa

Through consciousness, our minds have the power to change our planet and ourselves. It is time we heed the wisdom of the ancient indigenous people and channel our consciousness and spirit to tend the garden and not destroy it.

bruce lipton

By awakening the Native American teachings, you come to the realization that the earth is not something simply that you build upon and walk upon and drive upon and take for granted.
It is a living entity.
It has **consciousness**.

edgar cayce

The searcher carries no food or clothes —just a blanket—and spends the time fasting and praying. Eventually, a vision comes, revealing what he or she is supposed to do in life. Upon returning from the vigil, the young person describes the revelation to the wise elder. Then the two go together to the medicine man so he can interpret its meaning for them. Finally, the tribe has a big ceremony to formally name the young person and reveal his or her life's mission.

Rolling Thunder
Native American medicine man

Call your spirit back or die

The prayers are always for giving thanks.
Then, at times, there are things we can
ask…But not for ourselves. We ask
when it's related to what we're supposed
to be doing,that we may be guided in the
right manner.

Mad Bear
Tuscarora medicine man

All life is conscious,
but it is not conscious of being conscious.

doug boyd
Rolling Thunder
Mad Bear

Look up to the Creator.
Talk to him, pour your heart out.
The answer will come.

Bear Heart
medicine man
Muskogee-Creek Nation

You are the dream
that the old ones dreamed.

madeline cerise baker
MHA Nation

Upon suffering beyond suffering: the Red Nation shall rise again and it shall be a blessing for a sick world. A world filled with broken promises, selflessness and separations. A world longing for Light again. I see a time of Seven Generations when all the colors of mankind will gather under the Sacred Tree of Life and the whole Earth will become one circle again…

crazy horse

May we be granted the wisdom to return
to the divine laws and instructions
revealed long ago, when the Creator,
through his love, gave us the gift of life.
This gift was meant equally for all, and
with no room for injustice, hatred and
greed today poisoning our world.

>Grandfather David
>Hopi Nation

Protect your spirit, because you are
in the place where spirits get eaten.

>john trudell
>@Indigenous Thought

It was our belief that the love of possessions is a weakness to overcome. Its appeal is to the material part, and if allowed its way, it will in time disturb one's spiritual balance. Therefore, children must early learn the beauty of generosity. They are taught to give what they prize most, that they may taste the happiness of giving.

ohiyesa wahpeton santee
sioux

Practice kindness all day to everybody and you will realize you're already in heaven now.

jack kerouac

Those who can truly laugh can endure. So magnificent, so magical, is this divine and harmonious universe, that even the greatest of students, thinkers, physicists, philosophers, students of theology and astronomers still are seeking answers to this great mystery. But our faith keepers tell us that gratitude is the beginning of knowledge and understanding.

>ted williams
> Iroquois elder of the Wolf Clan
> Tuscarora Nation

At night when the streets of your cities and villages will be silent, and you think them deserted, they will throng with the returning hosts that once filled and still love this beautiful land. The white man will never be alone. Let him be just and deal kindly with my people, for the dead are not powerless. "Dead" did I say? There is no death, only a change of worlds.

Chief Seattle

You have your way. I have my way.
As for the right way, the correct way,
and the only way, it does not exist.

nietzsche

Let the spirit out — discard all thoughts
of reward, all hopes of praise and fears
of blame, all awareness of one's bodily
self. And finally closing the avenues of
sense perception, let the spirit out,
as it will.

bruce lee

All that we are is a result of what
we have thought.

the dhammapada

Reality is built out of thought,
and our every thought begins to
create reality.

edgar cayce

Hateful and fearful thoughts create
a hateful and fearful reality.
Reality is not happening to us ~
we are happening to reality.

kabamur

There is an entire universe that exists
solely in your mind that is impossible
to completely share with another person.
You are a god onto yourself and
beautiful and cruel as you wish to be.
That is the realist shit ever.

@Expherience

Your highest spiritual attainment occurred the moment you were born. Everything after this point of birth celebrates the enlightened master you already are ~ in whatever form you seem to appear. This is the simplicity and immaculate glory of self-realization.

matt kahn

Know thyself, for in thyself is to be found all that there is to be known.

alice ann bailey

*I am what I am,
and that's all that I am.*

popeye

I'm exhausted from trying to believe
unbelievable things.

steven wright

Appreciation is the
magic formula you've been seeking.

abraham

*I now accept limitless abundance
from a limitless universe*

Law of attraction 101:

* Visualize it.
* Hold that thought for about 20 seconds
* Put some emotion behind it (excitement)
* Repeat the process until you truly **believe** it can be done.

Behave and act as if it's already done.

Then, Let it go…

deion page

The idea 'you are what you attract'
is an oversimplification of the nuance
of metaphysics. Interpreting why
you attracted something is an art.

@MaryamHasnaa

Next time you're afraid to share ideas,
remember someone once said in a meeting:
"Let's make a film with a tornado
full of sharks."

jon acuff

Cannabis can make you more creative. Here's how:

1. Cannabis connects abstract ideas
2. Cannabis enhances focus
3. Cannabis improves episodic memory retrieval
4. Cannabis encourages introspection
5. Cannabis improves pattern recognition
6. Cannabis enhances cerebral blood flow

[Ask if Cannabis is right for you.]

Each human must integrate all timelines and then move into enlightenment as a state of being before they leave earth's dimensional reality.

@Immortal Masters

Ascension: the return of evolving matter to pure form; dynamic awareness moving beyond the wheel of birth and death.

@Immortal Masters

Reality is beyond thought.

sri rama krishna
#that's goin up on the frig

Consciousness resides in the microtubules of the brain cells, which are the primary sites of quantum processing. Upon death, this information is released from your body, meaning that your consciousness goes with it.

sir roger penrose
#stillprocessingthis

Let's get high on deep conversations

Death is not extinguishing the light;
it is putting out the lamp because
the dawn has come.

rabindranath tagore

Every parting gives a foretaste of death,
every reunion a hint of the resurrection.

schopenhauer

I know beyond a shadow of a doubt
that there is no death the way we
understood it.
The body dies, but not the soul.

elisabeth kubler-ross

After your death you will be
what you were before your birth.

schopenhauer

I felt in need of a great pilgrimage,
so I sat still for three days.

kabir

All that is necessary to awaken to
yourself as the radiant emptiness of
spirit is to stop seeking something
more or better or different, and to
turn your attention inward to the
awake silence that you are.

adyashanti

Throw everything away,
forget about it all! You are learning
too much, remembering too much,
trying too hard…relax a little bit, give
life a chance to flow its own way,
unassisted by your mind and effort.

Stop directing the river's flow.

mooji

One who thinks he knows,
does not know; one who knows he
does not know, knows.

the upanishads

An unmistakable trait of every true
genius is their persistent awareness of
how much more there is to know.
And an unmistakable trait of every true
sage is their persistent awareness of how
much more there is to love.

mike dooley

…only when all props and crutches are
broken, and no cover from the rear offers
even the slightest hope of security, does it
become possible for us to experience an
archetype that up till then had lain hidden.

carl jung

To have a better understanding of consciousness you need to pay attention only to what is right here right now, in front of you. **The present is not the now. The now is what is and is timeless.** There is no need to be concerned with the remembered past or the anticipated future, they exist only as they are imagined. Disengage from time oriented thinking to free your Self from needless worry and distraction from what is.

nvsk, urban dictionary

We're the future of the past. whoa.

@onlyastoner

When setting out on a journey,
do not seek advice from those
who have never left home.

rumi

It is important to expect nothing,
to take every experience,
including the negative ones,
as merely steps on the path,
and to proceed.

ram dass

You are an explorer,
and you represent our species,
and the greatest good you can do is to
bring back a new idea, because our world
is endangered by the absence of good
ideas. Our world is in crisis because of the
absence of consciousness.

terence mcKenna

Your existence alone has altered the world.
You're more important than you know.

@ReverieHippie

We live in illusion, the appearance of
things, but there is a reality and we are
that reality. When you understand this, you
see that you are nothing, and being nothing,
you are everything. That's all there is.

kalu rinpoche

*Remember,
the entrance door to the sanctuary
is inside you.*

rumi

Enlightenment is the unaltered state
of consciousness.

adyashanti

Maybe the journey isn't so much about becoming anything. Maybe it's about un-becoming everything that isn't really you so you can be who you were meant to be in the first place.

ralph smart

It takes a huge effort to free yourself from memory.

paulo coelho

Your existential crisis takes an interesting turn when you realize you're the main character in a first person video game.

@small worlds

Every moment is a fresh new beginning, a wonderful inauguration of the great cosmic journey through the universe.
We can do whatever we want.
We can change reality at any moment.

russell brand

Consciousness
is a fascinating but elusive subject;
it is impossible to specify what it is,
what it does or why it evolved.
Nothing worth reading has been
written about it.

stuart sutherland

Consciousness resides in a field
surrounding the brain in another
dimension. The entire body is a conduit
and a collaborator with consciousness as
a feedback loop.

dr. dirk k.f. meijer

Door: "Why it's simply impassible."

Alice: "Why, don't you mean impossible?"

Door: "No, I do mean impassible *(chuckles)*. Nothing's impossible!"

    lewis carroll

Somebody throw me a blunt!

The only way to discover the limits of the possible is to venture beyond the possible into the impossible.

arthur c. clarke

The purpose of life is to familiarize oneself with this after-death body so that the act of dying will not create confusion in the psyche…People are so alienated from their own soul that when they meet their soul they think it comes from another star system.

terence mcKenna

Interestingly, Jung's experiences with the *SOUL* and the *soul* (Jung, 1961) left no doubt in him that though the *soul* used the body, it wasn't the same as the body, any more than the driver of a car is the same as the car.

Assagioli (1971) went further, declaring that the development of consciousness and will were the purpose of the *SOUL'S* extension of a *soul* to Earth in the first place.

elmer green

...to every man his own truth...
And so, perhaps, the truth winds
somewhere between the road to
Glastonbury,
Isle of the Priests, and the road to
Avalon, lost forever in the
mists of the summer sea.

marion zimmer bradley
The Mists of Avalon

Eternity is taken not to be an
infinite temporal duration
but the quality of timelessness.

wittgenstein

The Universe is not outside of you.
Look inside yourself:
everything that you want,
you already are.

rumi

My suggestion:
Do theta training ~ and begin
exploring a 'new' world of Mind,
outside your head…

elmer green

Real silence means
there is actually nowhere else
for the mind to go.

anandamayi ma

So, if you are too tired to speak
sit next to me because I, too,
am fluent in silence.

r. arnold

*Accept what comes from silence.
Make the best you can of it.
Of the little words that come
out of the silence, like prayers
prayed back to the one who prays,
make a poem that does not disturb
the silence from which it came.*

wendell berry

When we turn the mind inward,
god manifests as the inner
consciousness.

sri ramana maharshi

Voltaire said:
"God is a comedian playing
in front of an audience too
afraid to laugh."

obviously…

@tom rhodes

Seriousness is an accident of time.
It consists in putting too high a
value on time.In eternity there is
no time.Eternity is a mere moment,
just long enough for a joke.

hermann hesse
#Lifeiswhatyoubakeit

What if we can breathe in space but the government just tells us we can't so we don't try to escape.

@conspiracykeanu

me: "no one can hear you scream in space"

my lawyer: "you gotta stop saying weird shit to the judge, man."

@chuuch

Emotion is the chief source of all
becoming-conscious. There can be no
transforming of darkness into light and
of apathy into movement without emotion.

carl jung

*Sometimes I'll start a sentence
and I don't even know where it's going.
I just hope I find it along the way.*

What I'm speaking about is the awakening
of a love that makes whatever is
happening in oneself unimportant.
For such a person self-concern has
dropped out of the center of awareness.

adyashanti

Aaaaand…into the forest I go,
to lose my mind and find my Soul.

john muir

No man is an island, entire of itself;
every man is a piece of the continent,
a part of the main.
If a clod be washed away by the sea,
Europe is the less,
as well as if a promontory were,
as well as if a manor of thy friend's
or of thine own were:
any man's death diminishes me,
because I am involved in mankind,
and therefore never send to know
for whom the bell tolls;
it tolls for thee.

john donne

Rave on, John Donne.

van morrison

A life without inner contradiction
is either only half a life or else
a life in the Beyond, which
is destined only for angels.
But God loves human beings
more than the angels.

c. g. jung

There have been times that I thought
I couldn't last for long
But now I think I'm able to carry on
It's been a long, a long time coming
but I know a change is gonna come,

Oh yes it will.

sam cooke

yes it will.

To be continued…

COSMIC

CANNABIS

CONSCIOUSNESS

VOLUME II

www.ingramcontent.com/pod-product-compliance
Lightning Source LLC
Chambersburg PA
CBHW051801040426
42446CB00007B/465